What Should We
Think of
The Carnal Christian?

What Should We Think of The Carnal Christian?

ERNEST C. REISINGER

THE BANNER OF TRUTH TRUST

THE BANNER OF TRUTH TRUST
3 Murrayfield Road, Edinburgh EH12 6EL
P.O. Box 621, Carlisle, Pennsylvania 17013, USA

•

© *The Banner of Truth Trust*
First published 1978
Reprinted 1978
Reprinted 1981
Reprinted 1986
Reprinted 1992
Reprinted 1997

ISBN 0 85151 389 1

•

Printed and bound in Great Britain by
Howie and Seath Ltd, Peffermill Industrial Estate
Edinburgh, EH16 5UY

Introduction

Many who regularly occupy church pews, fill church rolls, and are intellectually acquainted with the facts of the gospel never strike one blow for Christ. They seem to be at peace with his enemies. They have no quarrel with sin and, apart from a few sentimental expressions about Christ, there is no biblical evidence that they have experienced anything of the power of the gospel in their lives. Yet in spite of the evidence against them, they consider themselves to be just what their teachers teach them - that they are 'carnal Christians'. And as carnal Christians they believe they will go to heaven, though perhaps not first-class, and with few rewards.

That something is seriously wrong in lives which reveal such features will readily be admitted by most readers of these pages; no argument is needed to prove it. But the *most* serious aspect of this situation is too often not recognized at all. The chief mistake is not the carelessness of these church-goers, it is the error of their teachers who, by preaching the theory of 'the carnal Christian', have led them to believe that there are three groups of men, - the unconverted man, the 'carnal Christian' and the 'spiritual Christian'.

My purpose in this booklet is to argue that this classification is wrong and to set out the positive, historic, and biblical answer to this 'carnal Christian' teaching. The argument from Church history is not unimportant, for it is a fact that less than two hundred years ago this teaching was unknown in the churches of North America, but I am concerned to rest my case on an honest statement of the teaching of the Bible. I have written after study, private meditation and prayer, and after using many of the old respected commentaries of another day, but my appeal is to the

Word of God and it is in the light of that authority that I ask the reader to consider all that follows.

I must also confess that I am writing as one who, for many years, held and taught the teaching which I am now convinced is erroneous and which has many dangerous implications. As one who has deep respect for many who hold this position, I am not going to attack personalities, but to deal with principles, and with the interpretation of the particular passages of Scripture on which the teaching is built.

In matters of controversy it must ever be kept in mind that a Christian's experience may be genuine even though his understanding of divine truth is tainted with error or ignorance. The opposite is also possible - a man's intellectual understanding may be good and his experience poor. I pray that if I am in error on this or any other doctrine I shall be corrected before I leave this world. I trust I am willing ever to be a learner of divine truth.

I know that one of my motives is the same as that of many who hold this erroneous view, namely, to advance biblical holiness and to seek to 'adorn the doctrine of God our Saviour'.

To accomplish my purpose it is of the greatest importance that the whole subject should be set on a proper foundation. I do not want to make a caricature of the view of others and then demonstrate success by tearing it apart. I shall also seek to avoid disproportionate and one-sided statements. The danger that we may 'darken counsel by words without knowledge' is still with us. I pray that this effort will elicit truth and that the existence of varied opinions will lead us all to search the Scriptures more, to pray more, and to be diligent in our endeavours to learn what is 'the mind of the Spirit'.

My greatest difficulty will be to achieve brevity because this subject is so closely related to, and interwoven with the main doctrine of the Bible, particularly with justification and sanctification, the chief blessings of the new covenant. The subject therefore involves a right understanding of what the gospel really is and what it does to a person when applied efficaciously by the Spirit. Our view of this matter will also affect our judgment of the relationship of the Ten Commandments to the Christian in the area of sanctification, and of the biblical doctrine of assurance.

Some of the fundamental questions which need to be faced are these:

1. Are we sanctified *passively*, that is, 'by faith' only, without obedience to the law of God and Christ? If sanctification is passive - a view represented by the slogan 'Let go and let God' - then how do we understand such apostolic statements as 'I fight', 'I run', 'I keep under my body', 'let us cleanse ourselves', 'let us labour', 'let us lay aside every weight'? Surely these statements do not express a passive condition, nor do they indicate that by one single act we may possess the experience of 'victory' and thus become spiritual and mature Christians.

2. Does an appeal to the so-called 'carnal Christian' to become a 'spiritual Christian' minimize the real conversion experience by magnifying a supposed second experience, by whatever name it may be called - 'higher life', 'deeper life', 'Spirit-filled life', 'triumphant living', 'receiving Christ as Lord, and not merely as Saviour', and so on? The words we read in 2 Corinthians 5:17, 'Therefore, if any man be in Christ, he is a new creature: old things are passed away; behold, all things are become new', do not refer to a second experience but rather to what happens when any *real* conversion occurs.

3. Has the 'spiritual Christian' finished growing in grace? If not, what is he to be called as he continues to grow in grace? Do we need to make yet another class whose members are the 'super-spiritual Christians' ?

4. Who is to decide who the carnal Christians are, and exactly what standard is to be used in determining this? Do the 'spiritual Christians' decide who the 'carnal Christians' are? Does a

church or preacher decide where the line is to be drawn that divides the two classes or categories? Since all Christians have sin remaining in them, and since they sin every day, what degree of sin or what particular sins classify a person as a 'carnal Christian'?

Do not all Christians sometimes act like natural men in some area of their lives?

Do not the *inward* sins, such as envy, malice, covetousness, lasciviousness (which includes immorality on the mental level) demonstrate carnality as much as do the outward and visible manifestations of certain other sins?

In Romans 8:1-9 there is a division stated, but it is not between carnal and spiritual Christians. It is a division between those who walk after the flesh (the unregenerate) and those who walk after the Spirit (they that are Christ's). There is no third category.

Again, in Galatians 5:17-24 we have only two classes or categories - those that do the works of the flesh and those that are led by the Spirit. There is no third or fourth class or group.

My purpose, then, in these pages is to contend that the division of Christians into two groups or classes is unbiblical. I want also to show the dangerous implications and present-day results of this teaching.

The interpretation that I will seek to establish is a result of studying the proven and respected commentators of former days, such as, Matthew Henry, Matthew Poole, John Gill, and John Calvin; and theologians such as Charles Hodge (of the old Princeton Seminary), James P. Boyce (founder of the first Southern Baptist Seminary), Robert L. Dabney (the great theologian of old Union Seminary, Virginia) and James H. Thornwell (distinguished Southern theologian who was Professor of Theology at Columbia, South Carolina). I have also examined the writings of John Bunyan and searched the old Confessions and Catechisms, such as The Heidelberg Catechism, and Westminster Confession (that mother of all Confessions), the Baptist Confession of 1689 (The London Confession, later known as the Philadelphia Confession), and the Declaration of Faith of the Southern Baptist Church. In all these sources there is not one trace of the belief that there are three classes of men. All of them have much to say about carnality in Christians, and about the biblical doctrine of sanctification and its relationship to justification, but there is no hint of the possibility of dividing men into 'unregenerate', 'carnal' and 'spiritual' categories. If the sources I have named had come across the 'carnal Christian' theory, I believe that with one voice they would have warned their readers, 'Be not carried away with divers and strange doctrines' (Heb. 13:9).

I confess that I take up my pen in this controversy with deep sorrow. Although the teaching that I wish to expose is so relatively new in the church, it is held by so many fine Christians, and taught by so many able and respected schools of the present day, that I can only approach my present undertaking with caution and anxiety.

We live in a day when there are so many books and such a variety of teaching on the subject of the Christian life that Christians are 'tossed to and fro', and liable to be 'carried about by every wind of doctrine' (Eph. 4:14). There is also the Athenian love of novelty and a distaste for the old, well-tested, and beaten paths of our forefathers. This excessive love of the new leads to an insatiable craving after any teaching which is sensational and exciting, especially to the feelings. But the old paths lead to a 'meek and quiet spirit' which the apostle Peter commends: 'But let it be the hidden man of the heart, in that which is not corruptible, even the ornament of a meek and quiet spirit, which is in the sight of God of great price' (1 Pet. 3: 4) .

The Issue in Controversy

At a church service that I attended recently, the preacher, a sincere minister, was expounding 1 Corinthians chapter 3, and he said to a large congregation, 'Now after you become a Christian you have another choice - either to grow in grace, follow the Lord and become a spiritual Christian, or to remain a babe in Christ and live like natural men.' He used 1 Corinthians 3:1-4 to state that there were three categories of men - the *natural* man, the *spiritual* man, and the *carnal* man. He described the carnal man as being like the natural man who was unconverted.

This is the essence of the 'carnal Christian' teaching. One reason why it is so widespread is that it has been popularized for many years in the notes of the *Scofield Reference Bible*. A statement from these notes will indicate the precise nature of the teaching: 'Paul divides men into three classes: "Natural" i.e. the Adamic Man, unrenewed through the new birth; "Spiritual" i.e. the renewed man as Spirit-filled and walking in the Spirit in full communion with God; "Carnal", "fleshly", i.e. the renewed man who, walking "after the flesh", remains a babe in Christ.'[1]

It is very important to observe the two main things in this Scofield note. First, the division of men into three classes; second, we are told that one of these classes of men comprises the 'carnal', the 'fleshly', 'the babe(s) in Christ', 'who walk after the flesh'. To 'walk' implies the *bent* of their lives; their leaning or bias is in one direction, that is, towards carnality.

One of the most common and popular presentations of this position is available in the form of a small tract which presents the teaching like this:

1 *Scofield Reference Bible*, pp. 1213, 1214.

'After you have invited Christ to come into your life, it is possible for you to take control of the throne of your life again. The New Testament passage, 1 Corinthians 2: 14-3:3, identified three kinds of people:

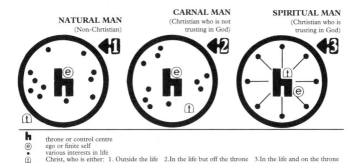

| **NATURAL MAN** | **CARNAL MAN** | **SPIRITUAL MAN** |
| (Non-Chrtistian) | (Chrtistian who is not trusting in God) | (Chrtistian who is trusting in God) |

h throne or control centre
ⓔ ego or finite self
• various interests in life
ⓕ Christ, who is either: 1. Outside the life 2.In the life but off the throne 3.In the life and on the throne

There will be no dispute about the first circle which represents the non-Christian. Note the position of the Ego, indicating that self is on the throne. The natural man is a self-centred man; his interests are controlled by self. Now compare this with the second circle - the only difference is that a cross (representing Christ) appears, although not on the throne. And the same little dots are in circle two as in circle one, indicating that there has been no basic reorganization or change in the nature and character. That is to say, the bent of the life of the 'carnal Christian' is the same as that of the non-Christian. Circle two gives basically the same picture as circle one, the only difference being that the 'carnal Christian' has made a profession of receiving Jesus. But he is 'not trusting God'.

A brief examination of this diagram and its interpretation of 1 Corinthians 3:1-4 will show that it is an accurate presentation of what wc have already found in the Scofield Bible notes.

We ought not to miss three very salient and important facts about the teaching:

First, we note again that it divides all men into three classes or categories. With this fact none of its proponents disagree, though they may present it differently and apply it differently.

Second, one class or category is set out as containing the 'Christian' who 'walks after the flesh'. The centre of his life is self, and he is the same as the unrenewed man as far as the bent of his life is concerned.

Third, all those who accept this view use 1 Corinthians 3:1-4 to support it. Consequently, if it can be established that the preponderance of Scripture teaches only two classes or categories of men - regenerate and unregenerate, converted and unconverted, those in Christ and those outside of Christ - the 'carnal Christian' teaching would be confronted with an insurmountable objection. It would be in conflict with the whole emphasis of Scripture and of the New Testament in particular.

Before I turn to some of the errors and dangers of the 'carnal Christian' teaching it may be wise to indicate what I am not saying.

In this discussion of the 'carnal Christian' theory I am not overlooking the teaching of the Bible about sin in Christians, about babes in Christ, about growth in grace, about Christians who back-slide grievously, and about the divine chastisement which all Christians receive.

I acknowledge that there are babes in Christ. In fact there are not only babes in Christ, but there are different stages of 'babyhood' in understanding divine truth and in spiritual growth.

I also recognize that there is a sense in which Christians may be said to be carnal but I must add that there are different degrees of carnality. Every Christian is carnal in some area of his life at many times in his life. And in every Christian 'the flesh lusteth against the Spirit' (Gal. 5:17).

All the marks of Christianity are not equally apparent in all Christians. Nor are any of these marks manifest to the same degree in every period of any Christian's life. Love, faith, obedience, and devotion will vary in the same Christian in different periods of his Christian experience; in other words, there are many degrees of sanctification. The Christian's progress in growth is not constant and undisturbed. There are many hills and valleys in the process of sanctification; and there are many stumblings, falls and crooked steps in the process of growth in grace.

There are examples in the Bible of grievous falls and carnality in the lives of true believers. Thus we have the warnings and the promises of temporal judgment and of chastisement by our heavenly Father.

These truths are all acknowledged and are not the point of this present discussion. The question we have to consider is: Does the Bible divide men into three categories? This is the issue at the heart of the 'carnal Christian' teaching.

*The teaching that I am opposing involves
nine serious errors:*

1. The misuse of 1 Corinthians 3

First: This 'carnal Christian' doctrine depends upon a wrong interpretation and application of 1 Corinthians 3:1-4, 'And I, brethren, could not speak unto you as unto spiritual, but as unto carnal, even as unto babes in Christ . . . are ye not carnal?' To understand the true meaning of these words it should be remembered that 1 Corinthians is not primarily a doctrinal epistle. Like all Scripture it contains doctrine, but it was not written - as was the Epistle to the Romans - to lay doctrinal foundations. Paul's immediate concern in writing this Epistle was to deal with practical problems in a young church. In the third chapter, and earlier, he is dealing with the danger of division arising out of a wrong esteem for those from whom they heard the gospel. They were looking at second causes and forgetting the God to whom alone all glory belongs. Instead of saying, 'We are Christ's disciples' and recognizing their union in him, they were forming parties and saying, 'We are Paul's for he founded the church in our city'; or 'Apollos is more eloquent than Paul and he edifies us more'; or, 'We are of Peter'. Thus opposing parties were set up.

It is important to see that the whole context is dealing principally with this one problem of unwholesome division. However, it has a common root with all the other problems in 1 Corinthians - the defrauding of one by another, the disorder at the Lord's Table, and so on. All the problems were the result of carnality, the outcome of that remaining principle of sin in all believers which Paul describes in Romans 7:21-23: 'I find then a law, that, when I would do good, evil is present with me. For I

10

delight in the law of God after the inward man: but I see another law in my members, warring against the law of my mind, and bringing me into captivity to the law of sin which is in my members.'[1]

In endeavouring to understand how Paul thinks of those he addresses in 1 Corinthians 3 we must bear in mind the designation he gives to them in chapter 1. He says they are 'sanctified in Christ Jesus', they are recipients of 'the grace of God', enriched by Christ 'in all utterance, and in all knowledge' (1:2-5). They are rebuked in chapter 3, not for failing to attain to privileges which some Christians attain to, but for acting, despite their privileges, like babes and like the unregenerate *in one area of their lives.*

This is very different from saying that the Apostle here recognizes the existence of a distinct group of Christians who can be called 'carnal'. When Paul comes to speak of classes, he knows only two, as is clear in chapter 2 of this same Epistle where he divides men into 'natural' and 'spiritual', and says, 'But the natural man receiveth not the things of the Spirit of God: for they are foolishness unto him: neither can he know them, because they are spiritually discerned. But he that is spiritual judgeth all things, yet he himself is judged of no man' (1 Cor. 2:14-15). Under the term *natural* the Apostle includes all those persons who are not partakers of the Spirit of God. If the Spirit of God has not given to them a new and higher nature then they remain what they are by their natural birth, namely, *natural* men.

The *spiritual* may be but babes in grace and babes in knowledge. Their faith may be weak. Their love may be in its early bud, their spiritual senses may be but little exercised, their faults may be many; but if 'the root of the matter' is in them and if

[1] For a clear and easily read exposition of this passage see Geoffrey B. Wilson *Romans*, a Digest of Reformed Comment, 1977, pp. 117-126, or, more fully, John Murray, *The Epistle to the Romans,* 1960.

they have passed from death unto life - passed out of the region of nature into that which is beyond nature - Paul puts them down in another class. They are all spiritual men although in some aspects of their behaviour they may temporarily fail to .appear as such.

Certainly these Christians at Corinth were imperfectly sanctified, as indeed are all Christians to a greater or lesser degree. But Paul is not saying that they were characterized by carnality in every area of their lives. He is not expounding a general doctrine of carnality but reproving a *specific* out-cropping of carnality in one certain respect. When Paul does state a foundational truth respecting the position of all Christians it is in such words as, 'If any man be in Christ, he is a new creature', and for all who are 'in Christ' it is also true that, 'old things are passed away; behold, all things are become new' (2 Cor. 5:17). There is no place for two classes of Christians in Paul's letter to the church at Corinth, and indeed no place for it anywhere in the teaching of Scripture. To interpret 1 Corinthians 3:1-4 in such a way as to divide men into three classes is to violate a cardinal rule for the interpretation of Scripture, namely, that each single passage must be interpreted in the light of the whole. It was a wise saying of one of the church fathers, 'If you have one Scripture only on which to base an important doctrine or teaching you are most likely to find, on close examination, that you have none'.

2. New covenant blessings are separated

Second: The 'carnal Christian' teaching divides the two basic blessings of the new covenant because it denies that one of them is experienced by all true Christians. Let me point out how basic the covenant is to Christianity. Jesus was the *mediator of the new covenant* - Hebrews 8:6-10: 'But now hath he obtained a more excellent ministry, by how much also he is the mediator of a better covenant, which was established upon better promises'.

The New Testament preachers were *ministers of the new covenant* - 2 Corinthians 3:5, 6: 'Not that we are sufficient of ourselves to think anything as of ourselves; but our sufficiency is of God; who also hath made us able ministers of the new testament (A.S.V. new covenant); not of the letter, but of the spirit: for the letter killeth, but the spirit giveth life.'

Every time we come to the Lord's table we are reminded of *the blessings of the new covenant* - Luke 22:20, 'This cup is the new covenant in my blood . . .'

These facts are enough to establish the importance of the new covenant. But what are the two blessings of the new covenant? The answer is clearly seen in many scriptural statements:

'Behold, the days come, saith the Lord, that I will make a new covenant with the house of Israel and with the house of Judah . . . I will put my law in their inward parts, and write it in their hearts. . . . I will forgive their iniquity, and will remember their sin no more' (Jer. 31:31-34).

'For I will take you from among the heathen, and gather you out of all countries, and will bring you into your own land. Then will I sprinkle clean water upon you, and ye shall be clean: from all your filthiness, and from all your idols, will I cleanse you. A new heart also will I give you, and a new spirit will I put within you: and I will take away the stony heart out of your flesh, and I will give you an heart of flesh. And I will put my spirit within you, and cause you to walk in my statutes, and ye shall keep my judgments, and do them' (Ezek. 36:24-27).

'Whereof the Holy Ghost also is a witness to us: for after that he had said before, This is the covenant that I will make with them after those days, saith the Lord, I will put my laws into their hearts, and in their minds will I write them; and their sins and iniquities will I remember no more' (Heb. 10:15-17) .

It is important to note that this is one covenant with two inseparable parts - *the forgiveness of sins* and *a changed heart*.

When a sinner is reconciled to God something happens in the record of *heaven*, the blood of Christ covers his sins. Thus, the first blessing is the forgiveness of sins. But at the same time something happens on earth in the *heart,* a new nature is given.

From the above Scriptures we also learn that Christ purchased the benefits and blessings of the new covenant. And the Epistle to the Hebrews reminds us that the gospel which the apostles preached as the gospel of Christ was the gospel of the new covenant. Therefore, whatever else sinners may receive when they are savingly called by the gospel, they must come into the primary blessings of the new covenant, namely, the forgiveness of sins *and* a new heart.

Well, what is the forgiveness of sins? It is an essential part of the justification of a man before God. And what is a new heart? It is nothing less than sanctification begun. But the 'carnal Christian' teaching appeals to those who are supposed to be justified, *as though* a new heart and life are optional. Sanctification is spoken of as though it can be subsequent to the forgiveness of sins and so people are led to believe that they are justified even though they are not being sanctified !

The truth is that we have no reason to believe that Christ's blood covers our sins in the record of heaven if the Spirit has not changed our hearts on earth. These two great blessings are joined together in the one covenant. The working of the Spirit and the cleansing of Christ's blood are inseparably joined in the application of God's salvation. Hence the teaching which calls for an act of submission or surrender (or whatever else it may be called) subsequent to conversion in order that the convert may live the spiritual life, cuts the living nerve of the new covenant. It separates what God has joined together.[1]

[1] For a further examination of this, see B. B. Warfield, *Perfectionism, 1958*, pp. 355—9.

3. Saving faith and spurious faith are not distinguished

The third major error is that this teaching does not distinguish between true, saving belief and the spurious belief which is mentioned in the following Scriptures: 'Many believed in his name ... But Jesus did not commit himself to them' John 2:23, 24. 'Many believed on him; but because of the Pharisees they did not confess him' John 12:42, 43. 'These have no root, which for a while believe' Luke 8:13. Simon Magus 'believed' and was baptized but his heart was 'not right in the sight of God' Acts 8:12-22. In other words, it was 'belief' without a changed heart and because this was Simon's condition Peter says he would perish unless he came to true repentance: he was 'in the gall of bitterness and in the bond of iniquity' (v 23). And the evidence that Simon Magus was indeed unsaved can be seen in his prayer. He, like all unregenerate people, was only concerned with the *consequence* of sin and made no request to be pardoned and cleansed from the impurity of sin. 'Pray ye,' he says to Peter, 'to the Lord for me, that none of these things which ye have spoken come upon me'. Like the so-called 'carnal Christian' he wanted Jesus as a kind of hell-insurance policy but he did not ask for deliverance from sin!

In all these scriptural instances men 'believed'; they had 'faith', but it was not saving faith. And all 'carnal Christians' profess their faith but it is not always saving faith.

Charles Hodge, following the Scriptures, makes a clear distinction between the different kinds of faith, (1) Speculative or dead faith, (2) temporary faith, (3) saving faith.[1]

Robert Dabney differentiates, (1) Temporary faith, (2) historical faith, (3) miraculous faith, (4) saving faith.[2]

The 'carnal Christian' teaching makes no allowance for these distinctions, it gives little or no recognition to the possibility of a

[1] *Systematic Theology,* Vol. 111, p. 68.
[2] *Lectures in Systematic Theology*, p. 600.

spurious belief, instead it implies or assumes that all who say they 'invite Jesus into their lives' are in possession of saving faith. If these professing believers do not live and act like Christians, their teachers may well say that it is because they are not 'spiritual Christians'. The fact is they may not be true believers at all !

4. The omission of repentance

A fourth flaw in the 'carnal Christian' teaching lies in its virtual exclusion of repentance from the conversion experience. This is implied by the suggestion that the 'carnal Christian' has not changed in practice but lives and acts just like the natural man. This teaching is obviously set forth in the diagram given above where self is still on the throne in the case of those in the second group. But thus to suggest that repentance, including a changed attitude to sin, is not an essential part of conversion is a very grave error. It is to depart from the apostolic gospel. No one who so minimizes the necessity of repentance can say with Paul, 'I kept back nothing that was profitable unto you, but have shewed you, and have taught you publicly, and from house to house, testifying both to the Jews, and also to the Greeks, repentance toward God and faith toward our Lord Jesus Christ' (Acts 20:20, 21).

John Cotton, one of the Puritan leaders of New England, was right when he wrote: 'There is none under a covenant of grace that dare allow himself in any sin; for if a man should negligently commit any sin, the Lord will school him thoroughly and make him sadly to apprehend how he has made bold with the treasures of the grace of God. *Shall we continue in sin that grace may abound? God forbid*: None that has a portion in the grace of God dareth therefore allow himself in sin; but if through strength of temptation he be at any time carried aside, it is his greatest burden'.[1]

[1] *A Treatise of the Covenant of Grace*, 1671 p. 89.

16

5. Wrong teaching on assurance

In the fifth place the three-class theory is prone to give assurance to those who were never really converted. When a person professes to belong to Christ and yet lives like the world, how do we know that his profession is genuine? How do we know it is not genuine? We don't! There are always two possibilities: he may be a true Christian in a condition of back-sliding, or it is quite possible he was never savingly united to Christ. Only God knows. Therefore when we speak of a back-slider two errors must be avoided: (1) Saying unequivocally that he is not a Christian; (2) Saying unequivocally that he is a Christian. The fact is that we do not know, we cannot know!

The Bible certainly teaches that to make men consider they are Christians when in reality they are not is a great evil, and insofar as the 'carnal Christian' theory allows for a whole category of 'Christians' whose hearts are not surrendered in obedience to Christ, its tendency is to promote that very evil. Nothing could be more dangerous. Lost, self-deceived souls who should be crying out to God for that supernatural change which is made known to themselves and to the world by a changed heart and life are often found hiding comfortably behind this very theory. As long as they believe it they will never seek a real salvation. Although they profess to hold evangelical truth their position is far worse than that of natural men who know that they are not converted!

The 'carnal Christian' teaching ignores much biblical teaching on the doctrine of assurance, especially those Scriptures which show that Christian character and conduct have a bearing on our assurance. The short First Epistle of John was written in order that those who believe may know that they have eternal life; that is, may know that they are born of God (5:13). Throughout the Epistle John stresses the marks that accompany the new birth (3:9; 5:18). He shows that a man born again is not at home in the realm of sin, and that disobedience to God's commandments *cannot* be the bent of a Christian's life, as the 'carnal Christian' teaching would lead us to believe. 'For whatsoever is born of God overcometh the world; and this is the victory that overcometh the world, even our faith' (5:4). 'And hereby we know that we know him, if we keep his commandments. He that saith, I know him, and keepeth not his commandments, is a liar, and the truth is not in him. But whoso keepeth his word, in him verily is the love of God perfected: hereby know we that we are in him' (2:3-5)

From such texts it is clear that obedience is intimately related to assurance; if we do not live and practise righteousness we have no reason to think that we are 'born of God'.[1]

Again, Jesus said, 'If you love me, keep my commandments,' (John 15:10) not, 'To be a spiritual Christian keep my commandments', for obedience is for *all* disciples. 'Follow holiness, without which no man shall see the Lord' (Heb. 12:14). 'Though he were a Son, yet learned he obedience by the things which he suffered; and being made perfect, he became the author of eternal salvation unto all them that *obey* him' (Heb. 5:8, 9). 'But as he which hath called you is holy, so be ye holy in all manner of conversation, because it is written, Be ye holy; for I am holy' (1 Peter 1: 15, 16).

The Bible makes it crystal clear that there is a close relationship between assurance and obedience; but the 'carnal Christian' teaching gives assurance to those who are at home in the realm of sin. They are classed as *Christians*. Many times this is a false and damning assurance because such have no biblical reason to believe that they are Christians at all.

[1] I am here dealing with the Antinomian error. An error on the opposite side is to make holiness and obedience the *ground* of our assurance, instead of the work of Christ, for the Holy Spirit witnesses to Christ as the sole ground of our peace and hope. But the same Spirit who gives assurance works *obedience* in the life, and therefore a faith in Jesus which is not attended by sanctifying power is not of God: 'Every man that hath this hope in him purifieth himself, even as he is pure' (1 John 3:3).

6. A low view of sin

Sixth: The fruits of this teaching are not new to Christianity even though the teaching appears on the present scene under a new mask. It is the old doctrine of Antinomianism. Paul attacks this in Romans 6:1, 2 when he asks, 'What shall we say then? Shall we continue in sin that grace may abound? God forbid . . .' By implication, the answer of the three-category teaching to Paul's question is, 'Yes, you can continue in sin and be a carnal Christian'. And that is Antinomianism!

7. A second work-of-grace made necessary

Seventh: 'carnal Christian' teaching is the mother of many second work-of-grace errors in that it depreciates the biblical conversion experience by implying that the change in the converted sinner may amount to little or nothing. It goes on to say that *the* important change which affects a man's character and conduct is the second step which makes him a 'spiritual Christian'.

8. A wrong view of Christ

Eighth: The 'carnal Christian' teaching is also the mother of one of the most soul-destroying teachings of our day. It suggests that you can take Jesus as your Saviour and yet treat obedience to his lordship as *optional.* How often is the appeal made to the so-called 'carnal Christians' to put Jesus on the throne and 'make him Lord'! When they accept Jesus as Lord, they are told, they will cease to be 'carnal Christians'. But such teaching is foreign to the New Testament. When our Lord appeared in human form in history the angel announced his coming in the words, 'For unto you is born this day in the city of David a Saviour, which is Christ the Lord' (Luke 2:11). He cannot be divided. The Saviour and Lord are one. When the apostles preached they proclaimed Christ to be Lord. To bow to his rule was never presented in the Bible as a second step of consecration. 'For we preach not ourselves, but Christ Jesus *the Lord;* and ourselves your servants for Jesus' sake' (2 Cor. 4: 5).

When sinners truly receive him they do receive him as Lord. 'As ye have therefore received Christ Jesus *the Lord,* so walk ye in him' (Col. 2: 6).

Matthew Henry, in his Introduction to the Gospel according to Matthew said: 'All the grace contained in this book is owing to Jesus Christ as our Lord and Saviour; and, unless we consent to him as our Lord we cannot expect any benefit by him as our Saviour.'

Charles Haddon Spurgeon warned his students: 'If the professed convert distinctly and deliberately declares that he knows the Lord's will but does not mean to attend to it, you are not to pamper his presumption, but it is your duty to assure him that he is not saved. Do not suppose that the Gospel is magnified or God glorified by going to the worldlings and telling them that they may be saved at this moment by simply accepting Christ as their Saviour, while they are wedded to their idols, and their hearts are still in love with sin. If I do so I tell them a lie, pervert the Gospel, insult Christ, and turn the grace of God into lasciviousness.'

It is vital in this connection to notice how the apostles preached the lordship of Christ. The word 'Saviour' occurs only twice in the Acts of the Apostles (5:31; 13:23), on the other hand the title 'Lord' is mentioned 92 times, 'Lord Jesus' 13 times, and 'The Lord Jesus Christ' 6 times in the same book! The gospel is: 'Believe on the *Lord* Jesus Christ and thou shalt be saved.'

It is the 'carnal Christian' teaching that has given rise to this erroneous teaching of the divided Christ. When Peter preached what we might call the first sermon after our Lord's ascension he made it abundantly clear that *we* do not make Christ Lord at all:

'Therefore let all the house of Israel know assuredly, that God hath made that same Jesus, whom ye have crucified, both Lord and Christ' (Acts 2:36). God has made him Lord! 'For to this end Christ both died, and rose, and revived, that he might be Lord of the dead and living' (Rom. 14:9). And the same grace which saves brings sinners to recognize this. But the three category teaching invites 'carnal Christians' to make Christ Lord and thus become spiritual Christians. Again, we see that this is treating our acceptance of his lordship as something additional to salvation, when, in fact, recognition of him as Lord is an integral and necessary part of conversion. A. A. Hodge has written:

'You cannot take Christ for justification unless you take him for sanctification. Think of the sinner coming to Christ and saying, "I do not want to be holy;" "I do not want to be saved from sin;" "I would like to be saved in my sins;" "Do not sanctify me now, but justify me now." What would be the answer? Could he be accepted by God? You can no more separate justification from sanctification than you can separate the circulation of the blood from the inhalation of the air. Breathing and circulation are two different things, but you cannot have the one without the other; they go together, and they constitute one life. So you have justification and sanctification; they go together, and they constitute one life. If there was ever one who attempted to receive Christ with justification and not with sanctification, he missed it, thank God! He was no more justified than he was sanctified.'[1]

9. False spirituality

Ninth: This teaching breeds Pharisaism in the so-called 'spiritual Christians' who have measured up to some man-made standard of spirituality. There ought to to be no professed 'spiritual

1 *Evangelical Theology*, Banner of Truth Trust, reprint 1976, pp.310-11.

Christians', much less 'super-spiritual' ones! George Whitefield, a man who lived very close to his Saviour, prayed all his days, 'Let me begin to be a Christian.' And another Christian has truly said: 'In the life of the most perfect Christian there is every day renewed occasion for self-abhorrence, for repentance, for renewed application to the blood of Christ, for application of the rekindling of the Holy Spirit'.

Conclusion

The effect of believing the truth set out in these pages ought to be that we long to see more true evangelism.

The 'carnal Christian' teaching is, after all, the consequence of a shallow, man-centred evangelism in which decisions are sought at any price and with any methods. When those pronounced to be converts do not act like Christians, do not love what Christians love, and hate what Christians hate, and do not willingly serve Christ in his church, some explanation must be found other than calling upon them to 'decide' for Christ. They have already done that and have already been pronounced by the preacher or personal worker to be 'Christians'. But when they don't act like Christians something is wrong. What is it? The teaching I have sought to answer says that the trouble is that they are just 'carnal Christians'; they have not made Christ 'Lord' of their lives; they have not let him occupy the throne of their hearts. Once this explanation is seen to be unscriptural it will also be seen to be closely connected with an initial error over evangelism itself. Too often, modern evangelism has substituted a 'decision' in the place of repentance and saving faith. Forgiveness is preached without the equally important truth that the Spirit of God must change the heart. As a result decisions are treated as conversions even though there is no evidence of a supernatural work of God in the life.

Surely the best way to end this evil is to pray and labour for the restoration of New Testament evangelism! Whenever such evangelism exists it is certain that men will learn that it is not enough to *profess* to be a Christian, and not enough to *call* Jesus 'Lord, Lord' (Luke 6:46). The gospel preached in awakening power will summon men not to rest without biblical evidence that they are born of God. It will disturb those who, without good reason, have believed that they are already Christians. It will arouse backsliders by telling them that as long as they remain in that condition the possibility exists that they never were genuine believers at all. And to understand this will bring new depths of compassion and urgency to the hearts of God's people in this fallen world.

One of the greatest hindrances to the recovery of such preaching is the theory we have considered. To reject that theory is to be brought back to a new starting-point in evangelism and in the understanding of the Christian life. It is to bring God's work into the centre of our thinking. It is to see afresh that there are only two alternatives - the natural life or the spiritual life, the broad way or the narrow way, the gospel 'in word only' or the gospel 'in power and in the Holy Ghost' (1 Thess. 1:5), the house on the sand or the house on the rock.

There is no surer certainty than the fact that an unchanged heart and a worldly life will bring men to hell. 'Let no man deceive you with vain words: for because of these things cometh the wrath of God upon the children of disobedience' (Eph. 5: 6).

It is not only in the world today that evangelism is needed. It is needed in the church.

For further reading

The Works of John Owen, vol. 6, On Mortification of Sin; Temptation; and Indwelling Sin in Believers. Banner of Truth Trust.
Holiness, J. C. Ryle, James Clarke.
The Sermon on the Mount, D. M. Lloyd-Jones, Inter-Varsity Press.
Romans, A Digest of Reformed Comment, G. B. Wilson, Banner of Truth Trust.

Some other
Banner of Truth Titles

TODAY'S GOSPEL:
Authentic or Synthetic?
Walter Chantry

In this arousing work Walter Chantry expounds from Christ's dealing with the Rich Young Ruler the essential elements in Gospel preaching. A close examination of the Scriptural evidence leads to this conclusion:

'Differences between much of today's preaching and that of Jesus are not petty; they are enormous. The chief errors are not in emphasis or approach but in the heart of the Gospel message. Were there a deficiency in one of the areas mentioned in these pages, it would be serious. But to ignore all - the attributes of God, the holy law of God, repentance, a call to bow to the enthroned Christ - and to pervert the doctrine of assurance, is the most vital mistake.

'Incredulity may grip you. Can so many evangelicals be so wrong? . . . All are not in error, but great hosts are. All have not perverted the gospel to the same degree, but many are terribly far from the truth. All those who "make decisions" are not deceived, but great numbers are. Above all, few *care* to recover the Gospel message . . .'

This powerfully-written book has a message which goes to the heart of the contemporary problem in a way that conferences and commissions on evangelism have failed to. do. Its expository approach is particularly valuable.

ISBN 0 85151 027 2
96pp, Paperback.

FAITH: THE GIFT OF GOD
Tom Wells

Two men hear the gospel. They are from similar backgrounds, one turns to faith in Christ; the other turns away from Christ. Why the difference? Faith in the one, unbelief in the other! But how does faith come? Answers vary considerably. Some lay emphasis on God's work; others stress man's action. Many imply that a doctrinal understanding of the problem does not matter.

In this book Tom Wells shows us that it certainly matters. He invites us (1) to search into the Scriptures which bear on the matter and (2) to look back and examine our own coming to faith in Christ. Under the blessing of the Holy Spirit this should help our whole understanding of the doctrines of God, man and salvation.

The conclusion that the faith with which we believe is only ours because God creates it in our heart arises from man's evil nature and God's holy character. No man left to himself will ever turn to Christ. Nor will God share his glory with another. Salvation is all of grace. Faith *is* the gift of God.

This book is a refreshingly new approach to a Biblical understanding of the doctrines of faith and salvation. It is an attempt 'to write theology for the ordinary man'.

ISBN 0 85151 361 1
160pp, Paperback.

For free illustrated catalogue please write to:

THE BANNER OF TRUTH TRUST
3 Murrayfield Road, Edinburgh EH12 6EL
P.O. Box 621, Carlisle, Pennsylvania 17013, USA